ISBN 978-1-331-38859-3
PIBN 10183284

This book is a reproduction of an important historical work. Forgotten Books uses
state-of-the-art technology to digitally reconstruct the work, preserving the original format
whilst repairing imperfections present in the aged copy. In rare cases, an imperfection in
the original, such as a blemish or missing page, may be replicated in our edition. We do,
however, repair the vast majority of imperfections successfully; any imperfections that
remain are intentionally left to preserve the state of such historical works.

1 MONTH OF
FREE
READING

at
www.ForgottenBooks.com

By purchasing this book you are eligible for one month membership to ForgottenBooks.com, giving you unlimited access to our entire collection of over 700,000 titles via our web site and mobile apps.

To claim your free month visit:

www.forgottenbooks.com/free183284

Similar Books Are Available from
www.forgottenbooks.com

IGIN..AND
LL OF THE ALAMO

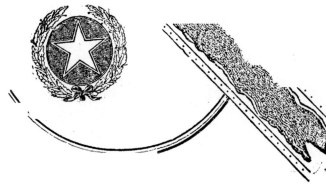

March,
A. D. 1836.

••••

COL. JNO. S. FORD, Author.

THE ALAMO.

ORIGIN AND

FALL OF THE ALAMO

MARCH 6, 1836.

By John S. Ford,

One of a Committee of the Alamo Association.

1896;
JOHNSON BROTHERS PRINTING COMPANY,
San Antonio, Texas.

The Committee, appointed to prepare a History of the Alamo, report as follows:

In treating of the Alamo it is due to the people of Texas to give, at least, a short account of the settlement of Americans in Texas, and of the causes leading to the revolution of 1835 and 1836. There were Americans in Texas previous to the advent of Moses Austin, December, 1820. Anterior to this period of time Americans had entered Texas with a view of assisting the revolutionists in the war they were waging against the King of Spain. They effected good service on several occasions. In the interior portions of Mexico Americans rendered considerable aid to the Mexicans. The United States in throwing off the yoke of England was an example many States in America endeavored to imitate. The effect of these causes gave to Americans a distinguished consideration. It was, no doubt, one of the main inducements causing a favorable answer to be made to Moses Austin when he applied for authority to introduce settlers into Texas. This authority was granted in 1821.

It must be remembered that La Salle had entered Texas in 1685, and had made a settlement of Frenchmen, and had built Fort St. Louis, on the Lavacca river. This fact, with others of a later date, induced the Viceroy of Mexico, the Duke of Linares, to take steps for the permanent occupation of Texas. He sent Don Domingo Ramon with troops, and a party of Franciscan friars to civilize and christianize Indians. This occurred in 1715. Ramon established some forts and missions. He located a fort, or *presidio* as the Spaniards call them, on San Pedro creek, three-fourths of a mile from the public square of the city of San Antonio. The name given to this *presidio* was San Antonio de Valero. In 1718 the Franciscans established a mission at this place. It was removed on more than one occasion, and was located on what is now the Military plaza of San Antonio. From there it was removed, in 1718, to its present site, the east bank of the San Antonio river, and is known as the church of the Alamo. It received a supply of water by means of the Alamo ditch—

Acequia Madre del Alamo. The erection of the church was commenced in 1716. It faces to the west. There were other buildings connected with the church. East of the church stood the Convent, 191 feet in length; it ran north to the south line of East Houston street. There was an enclosure north of the Convent yard. There were houses attached to the mission, which had been inhabited. Outside of the mission were houses occupied, at one time by christianized Indians. They abandoned them when the Texians took possession of the Alamo. It was in these houses that the Texians found eighty or ninety bushels of corn. The walls of the Alamo and the adjoining building were too extensive to be occupied and defended by 150 men.

After the death of Moses Austin, his son, Stephen F. Austin, proceeded to carry into effect the introduction of settlers into Texas.

Great attention to Texas had been drawn by the reports of men who had been engaged with officers who had entered Texas to aid the Mexicans in achieving their independence. It was known that Mexico was encouraging emigration. When Austin visited the City of Mexico, he found a number of influential gentlemen asking for permission to become *empresarios*, that is, to become leaders of immigrants. They were offered, and, as a rule, received a grant of land for the introduction of each person. Austin succeeded, and began his settlements on the Brazos river. Other gentlemen were also successful. The country began to fill up with settlers. It was full of Indians, who were opposed to the introduction of white people. They waged an incessant and cruel war upon the Texians.

The leaders in Mexico became jealous of the accession of Americans as citizens. They evinced their opposition by acts of oppression. The American settlers had sworn to obey and support the Mexican constitution of 1824. By several acts of Gen. Santa Anna indicating his intention to assume the dictatorial position the people of Texas became assured of his intention to overthrow the constitution of 1824. The people of Texas had given the Mexican government some very convincing proofs of their intention not to submit to the exercise of any illegal and tyrannical acts against them.

The government of the United States had proposed to pay the Mexican government $4,000,000 for Texas. This proposition

angered the Mexicans and increased their antipathy to **Texians.**
They began to persecute them by sending troops, not to chastise
Indians, but to check and punish **Texians** for their adhesion to
correct and liberal principles.   These military aiders of tyranny
were expelled from Texas.   One of these envoys of a despotic
president was an American by birth, Col. Bradburn.   He robbed
Texians, and made prisoners of William B. Travis, Patrick H.
Jack and Monroe Edwards.   The Texians embodied, elected Col.
Francis W. Johnson to command.   By their representations to
Col. Piedras, commander at Nacogdoches, Col. Bradburn was
removed from Texas.   This event took place in 1831.   Bradburn
was posted at Anahuac.   On June 25th Capt. John Austin, at
the head of sixty men, defeated Lt.-Col. Ugartechea, at Fort
Velasco.   He had 125 men.   August 2, 1832, Col. James W.
Bullock defeated Col. Piedras at Nacogdoches.   These affairs
took place while President Bustamente was in power in Mexico.
The Texians took sides with Santa Anna at that time.   He was
beaten by Gen. Santa Anna, who succeeded to the presidency of
Mexico.   The people of Texas, reposing confidence in Santa
Anna, declared for him.   He had been one of the heroes in the
Mexican struggle for independence.   He soon undeceived them;
became dictator; overthrew the constitution of 1824, and issued
an order for the disarming of the people—one man out of every
five hundred was allowed to own a fire lock.   On May 16, 1833,
Santa Anna took his seat as President of Mexico.   At that date
Stephen F. Austin was a prisoner in the City of Mexico.   Austin
had belonged to a convention to form a constitution for Texas.
That body elected Austin, W. H. Wharton and Miller to present
to the President of Mexico a statement of affairs in Texas.   It
was written by David G. Burnet, afterwards President of Texas.
Stephen F. Austin was the only person who visited Mexico.
This was in March, 1833.   Santa Anna, at that time, had retired
from the Mexican capitol.   He was scheming to effect the work
he afterwards performed, that is, to be made President under
laws he dictated.   He, after various trials to have Austin
condemned by the court, allowed him to return to Texas.   He
arrived in September, 1835.

   Col. Austin found the people of Texas in great excitement.
They had discovered that Santa Anna was unfriendly to them.
The municipalities of different sections had held public meetings,

and announced their intention to support the Mexican constitution of 1824. It must be remembered that the Indians had made war upon them, and they were compelled, as a measure of personal safety, to carry arms at all times. Circumstances made them watchful and efficient soldiers. War was forced upon them ; necessity caused them to bear arms ; God had implanted in their natures the principles of honor and integrity ; and practice had converted them into heroes in the cause of right.

The Texians appealed to their fellow citizens of Mexico without effect. They used every effort in their power to prove their disposition to be peaceful and useful citizens of the Republic of Mexico. It was all of no avail. In 1834 Santa Anna determined to send 4,000 troops to San Antonio. He sent Colonel Juan N. Almonte into Texas ; as a spy, no doubt. On October 13, 1834, the first revolutionary meeting in Texas was held at San Antonio. They approved the calling of a convention at that place, to meet November 15. This motion was made by Don Erasmo Seguin. October 20th another meeting was held at San Felipe. They proposed the dissolution of Texas from the State of Coahuila.

In January, 1835, the Congress of Mexico met. The State of Zacetecas had declared for the constitution of 1824. The Congress declared Zacetecas in a state of rebellion. This induced General Santa Anna to head 3,400 men to march into Zacetecas. May 10, 1835, Don Francisco Garcia, at the head of 5,000 troops, was defeated by Santa Anna. The City of Zacetecas was delivered to the Mexican soldiers, and was plundered for two days. The people of Texas now saw what they might expect from President Santa Anna. General Cos, a brother-in-law of Santa Anna, was ordered from Matamoros to Monclova to disperse the legislature of Coahuila, which he accomplished.

Meantime, the people were preparing to meet the coming war. The municipalities resolved to do their duty. In July, 1835, Lorenzo de Zavala, late Governor of the State and City of Mexico, arrived in Texas. He was made Minister to France, but fled from Santa Anna. The Texians formed committees of public safety. July 17, 1835, there was a meeting of representatives of the municipalities of Austin, Columbia and Mina, held at San Felipe. They did some good.

The Mexican forces were expected in October to aid in the change of government in Texas. Immigrants from the United

States, since the law of April 6, 1830, were to be driven from the country. A long list of proscribed Texians had been prepared. They were to be arrested and tried by drum-head court. Slaves were to be freed. *Empresarios* dismissed—none but emigrants from Mexico admitted. These were among the objects proposed to be accomplished. These intended changes spurred the Texians on to resistance.

In 1835 the command of Capt. Tenorio, at Anahuac, were captured by Col. Wm. B. Travis. The Texians of Columbus issued a call for '' a consultation of all Texas.'' It was dated August 20, 1835. Col. Ugartechea was removed from command, at Goliad, by Gen. Cos ; Col. Candelle took his place. He stripped Goliad of arms, forced the citizens to become soldiers, and ordered five soldiers to be quartered on each family. He placed the alcade in jail, and forced the *administrador* to hand over $5,000, under penalty of going to San Antonio in two hours, on foot. Gen. Cos reached San Antonio late in September, 1835.

In 1831 a piece of artillery had been furnished the town of Gonzales by the commandant at San Antonio. Ugartechea, in San Antonio, in 1835, sent a messenger to demand the cannon. It was refused. Cos ordered Capt. Castonado to take one hundred men and secure the cannon. He reached Gonzales September 29, 1835.

During the interval the committee of safety had sent runners to procure men. The men came. They numbered 168, and elected John H. Moore, Colonel, and J. W. E. Wallace Lieut.-Colonel. The Texians crossed the river Guadalupe, and firing occurred— some Mexicans reported killed. Capt. Castonado retreated. This affair opened the revolution.

The Texians felt the importance of united action and preparation. The committee of safety agreed to send one of their number from each municipality to San Felipe, for the purpose of procuring unity and concert in measures. Of this R. R. Royall was chosen president. The people of San Augustine nominated Gen. Sam Houston to command her troops. Nacodoches approved the suggestion. The money paid for land and custom-house dues was appropriated by the Texians. Efforts were made to secure arms and ammunition. The people were united. The spirit of '76 was in the ascendant. Less than 100,000 in population, threw down the gauntlet to an organized government of 8,000,-

ooo. They knew the penalty of failure was death in all its horrible forms.

The volunteers arrived daily at Gonzales. They made a proposition to defer the meeting of the consultation till November 1st. October 12th five hundred men crossed the Guadalupe river, destined for San Antonio. The resolution had been formed to drive every Mexican soldier out of Texas. Stephen F. Austin arrived at Gonzales October 10th. He was elected General. The fight at Mission Concepcion took place on October 28 The Texians numbered ninety, the Mexicans several hundred. Victory perched on the banner of the revolutionists.

The members of the consultation in the Texas army were permitted to proceed to San Felipe. The army besieged San Antonio. Gen. Austin was appointed to visit the United States to procure men and means. His colleagues were Dr. Branch T. Archer and W. H. Wharton. Edward Burleson was elected to command. On December 10, 1835, Gen. Cos surrendered.

The incidents of the siege of S in Antonio are worthy of notice. It was reported in the Texian camp that Col. Ugartechea was on his way with reinforcements for Gen. Cos. A force of Texians under Col. Bowie, with Deaf Smith as guide, was sent out to intercept Ugartechea. Gen. Cos had sent men out to obtain a supply of grass for his horses. They were on their return and about five miles from the city they were discovered. When they were within a mile of town the Texians, under Bowie, charged them. A fight ensued. The Mexicans were endeavoring to reach their headquarters. Gen. Cos detached reinforcements. The main body of the Texas troops came up. They charged, and the Mexicans continned to fight, though moving for town. Their loss was about fifty killed and a number wounded. The Texians had none killed, two wounded and one missing. They captured about seventy head of horses. This affair is known as the "Grass Fight." It occurred November 26, 1835.

Dr. Grant created trouble by advocating a campaign against Matamoros, Mexico. Two hundred and fifty were deluded into the belief that the Mexicans were ripe for driving Santa Anna out of Mexico. November 29th Grant was reported to have two hundred and fifty men ready to march to the Rio Grande. The annexed happenings, no doubt, prevented Dr. Grant from dividing the Texas force.

December 3, 1835, Messrs. John W. Smith, Holmes and Samuel Maverick entered the Texas lines. They had been detained by Gen. Cos since the affair at Gonzales. They reported the strength of the enemy as exaggerated. The idea of storming San Antonio had been suggested and advocated. It was popular. Meantime, about the 4th of December, Arnold, the Texas guide, had returned. Lieutenant Vuavis, of the Mexican army, had deserted, and was examined by Gen. Burleson. He reported dissatisfaction in the Mexican camp; that the strength in the city was much less than supposed. On the evening of that day Col. Benjamin R. Milam cried aloud, "Who will go with old Ben Milam to San Antonio?" There was a general shout of approval. The parties advocating the scheme assembled at Gen. Burleson's headquarters. They fell into line, and at once elected Milam to lead them. He directed them to meet him at the old mill at night to complete arrangements. Gen. Burleson and the whole command said the matter met their approbation. At the mills the attacking party was formed in two divisions. The first under the immediate command of Col. Milam, assisted by Col. Nidland Franks of the artillery, and Major R. C. Morris of the New Orleans Greys. Messrs. Maverick, Cooke and Arnold acted as guides. The second column was commanded by Col. Frank W. Johnson, assisted by Colonels James Grant and Wm. T. Austin, with Deaf Smith and John W. Smith as guides. Gen. Burleson agreed to hold his position until the result of the attack was known. Col. J. C. Neill was directed to make a feint upon the Alamo to direct the attention of the enemy, while the others were entering the town. The attacking party consisted of three hundred and one men. The companies of Captains York, Dickinson, English and Ward, composed the first division, under Colonel Milam, commander. The companies of Captains Cooke, Breese, Peacock, Swisher and Edwards, formed the second division under Col. Johnson.

Col. Neill performed his part. He opened fire on the Alamo, and drew the attention of the enemy to that quarter. When he heard the guns of Milam on the opposite side of the river he withdrew. Milam moved on Acequia street (Ditch street). Johnson entered Soledad street (Solitary street). These two streets run nearly south on parallel lines, and enter the Main square, the first at the northwest and the other at the northeast corner. At these points the enemy had erected works. Milam's division occupied

MISSION CONCEPCION

de la Garza's house, Johnson the Veramendi house. Both these houses were about one hundred yards from the Main square. The Veramendi house is still standing. The door on the street side shows signs where balls passed through. On approaching the Veramendi house a sentinel fired on the Texians. He was killed by Deaf Smith. Upon this, the Mexicans began a furious firing from the town and the Alamo. A twelve-pounder and a six-pounder accompanied the two divisions. The twelve-pounder was soon dismounted, and the six-pounder made about useless. The Texians covered themselves with difficulty. They soon opened fire with their rifles, and silenced all the artillery within their reach. The fight continued during the day. The Texians established communication between the two divisions. That day, the 5th of December, they lost one man killed and twelve wounded. Among the wounded were Lieutenants Hall and Deaf Smith.

During the night the enemy kept up a continuous fire. They placed men on tops of houses in their possession. They cut loopholes in the parapet walls of the houses.

On the 6th the Mexicans kept up a steady fire of cannon and small arms. On that day Lieut. Wm. McDonald, of Capt. Crane's company, captured a house to the right and a little in advance of de la Garza's house. This extended the Texas line westwardly, and in direction of the Military Plaza. They strengthened their works and remounted their twelve-pounder. On this day they had five men wounded.

The morning of the third day the enemy fired briskly from a trench between the Alamo and the river. By 11 o'clock this fire was silenced, and that of some of the Mexican artillery. A house stood between the Garza house and the plaza buildings. This was entered by the gallant Karnes, crow-bar in hand, backed by the company of Captain York. They held the position. In the evening the fire of the Mexicans was brisk. Colonel Milam was killed at the back of the Veramendi house. He was buried near where he fell. Captain Swisher was present at the burial, and afterwards pointed out the exact spot. This was an incentive inducing Texians to strike for vengeance.

Yoakum says: They immediately set on foot a party to take possession of the house of Antonio Navarro, situated on the north side of the Main street, one block west of the Main plaza, but commanding a portion of the Military plaza, and the Mexican redoubt on the second block west of the main square. The party consisted of portions of the companies of Captains Llewyllen. English, Crane and York. They advanced from the house taken by Karnes, and forced an entrance. The enemy endeavored to retake it by firing through the loop-holes made in the roof; but the Texians returned the fire through the same loop-holes, and drove them off.

On the 8th of December the "Zambrano Row" was taken. The thick partition walls were penetrated by crow-bars. The fight was fierce and subborn, but the enemy were finally expelled. General Burleson sent a detachment under Lieutenant Gill to assist the Texians. The Mexicans attempted a diversion by sending a detachment of about fifty men in the direction of the Texas camp. They were forced to retire by the fire of a six-pounder. The occupants of the the "Zambrano Row" were reinforced by the companies of Captains Swisher, Alley, Edwards and Duncan. At this time the Texians had command of the northwest portion of the enemy's main defenses.

On December 8th, at night, a party of about one hundred Texians attacked the "Priest's House." It commanded the plaza. In approaching the building the men were subjected to a heavy fire. They moved rapidly, broke down the wall of an outbuilding, and drove the Mexicans from the "Priest's House." They cut loop-holes, and prepared to use their rifles with effect when daylight appeared. The enemy abandoned the square and retired to the Alamo.

On the morning of December 9th General Cos sent in a flag of truce, proposing to surrender. Cos had been reinforced by five hundred convicts, conducted by Col. Ugartechea. They were chained and guarded by one hundred infantry. They were a source of trouble and disquietude. In addition, there was a derth of provisions. The force of General Cos was estimated at 800 previous to the arrival of the "volunteers." After that his force consisted of 1,400 men. These he surrendered, December 10, 1835. He pledged that he and his men were not to fight against the Texians, unless exchanged. He was allowed to purchase provisions. He begun his march to Laredo on the 14th day of December, at the head of 1,105 troops. The balance were allowed to remain in obedience to terms of capitulation. The Mexican loss was about 150 killed. The Texian loss very small.

The disabled and sick Mexicans were allowed to remain, and were cared for by the victors.

Col. Johnson, the leader of the attacking party after the fall of Col. Milam, remained in command at San Antonio for a short while. He is now dead.

Gen. Edward Burleson returned to his home. He was afterwards Vice-President of the Republic of Texas. He died in the year 1851.

Samuel Maverick was a zealous, useful, and efficient friend of Texas. He was an able citizen, and filled many places of trust. He died several years since. He had the good will, and possessed the confidence of his fellow citizens.

The writer took account of the siege of San Antonio principally from Yoakum's history. He had no time to consult other accounts.

Mrs. Bradley deserves mention as one of the old-timed residents of San Antonio.

The consultation met November 1st. They consisted of 55 members. They elected Sam Houston General in Chief, Henry Smith Governor and James W. Robinson Lieutenant-Governor of Texas. They left one member from each municipality to assist the Governor in the discharge of his duties—about 15. These were not all present at one time; part of them went home, and returned. They differed with Governor Smith; quarrelled with him; assumed unqualified authority, and assumed to displace the Governor from office, electing J. W. Robinson Governor. All this was done without the sanction of law. These gentlemen were, no doubt, patriots. They appointed men to fill military offices, intending to invade Mexico. The Texians butchered at San Patricio, Refugio and Goliad, resulted from the action of the opponents of Governor Smith. General Houston attempted to concentrate the army, but his orders were not obeyed. This trouble was the cause of the failure to send men to reinforce Travis at the Alamo.

After the surrender of General Cos many of the Texians returned to their homes. A garrison was left at San Antonio, under command of Col. Neill. Dr. Grant revived his project of a campaign against Matamoros. He illegally took possession of winter clothing, ammunition, provisions, and in addition induced a large number of the garrison to follow him. He seized private property, without authority. He left and proceeded to San Patricio, where outside the town he was attacked by General Urrea, and his party all killed. His coadjutor, Colonel Frank W. Johnson was at San Patricio with men. They were surprised, defeated and many of them killed. General Urrea had moved from Matamoros. He destroyed the command of Colonel Fannin. They surrendered as prisoners, and the main portion of them were afterwards shot, by order of General Santa Anna, in violation of the rules of civilized warfare. The Alamo had previously fallen. The number of soldiers who had been sacrificed by the vaulting ambition of a few leaders, and the acts of a few members of the consultation, amounted to nearly one thousand. These, if they had obeyed General Houston's order to fall back, and concentrate, would have been able to meet Santa Anna on the outskirts of the settlements, beaten him, and secured peace.

After Dr. Grant had stripped San Antonio of men and means there was left of the garrison 150 men. They had been poorly paid. Col. Neill had received orders to burn the Alamo, destroy what he was unable to remove, and march to a designated place. He has never published his reason for disobedience of orders. He left, it is averred, to procure transportation for the arms, and public property, in the city. Deaf Smith accompanied him, which was a deprivation to the men of the garrison. About this time Colonel Travis arrived; he brought about thirty men. He assumed command of the regulars. Colonel Bowie commanded the volunteers. He had visited the different commands aiming to march into Mexico, and endeavored to persuade them to desist, and obey orders. He came to San Antonio; it was his home. After the departure of Deaf Smith there was no one the Texians placed confidence in who could inform them of the approach of General Santa Anna. He was expected, but no one knew when he would arrive. Colonel Seguin was in the employ of the Texians. He was afterwards in the battle of San Jacinto. He sent a relative to Laredo. He returned and reported General Santa Anna at Laredo, at the head of an army. The Texians would not believe him.

General Santa Anna proceeded up the Rio Grande to a point opposite Presidio Rio Grande, to effect a junction with troops coming from the State of Coahuila. At Laredo he met the retiring troops of General Cos. This command was forced to violate the terms of their surrender, and return to Texas. Santa Anna marched upon the road direct from Presidio Norte to San Antonio. Prairie fires had destroyed the grass. Sergeant Becerra, of Santa Anna's army, affirms that the members of a mounted regiment had to walk and lead their horses. The want of provender had rendered them unable to carry a soldier. General Santa Anna issued orders on the march, indicating his intention to treat Texians with the most relentless severity When the Mexican command reached the Medina, Sergeant Becerra said General Santa Anna was visited by a Mexican gentleman of San Antonio. Señor Navarro. The General asked questions about the Texians. He was informed there was a fandango in the city, and quite all the Texians were in attendance, no doubt. The General expressed an intention to move at once, and surprise them. A very heavy rain had fallen recently. The Medina was quite full. The army had camped on both sides the stream. The ammunition wagons were on the south side, and could not be passed over with apparent safety. There was no boat with the Mexican command. In a conversation, General Santa Anna is reported to have said, that the Mission of Concepcion was better calculated to be defended by a small party than the Alamo, and he anticipated the Texians would occupy it.

February 23, 1836, the Mexican army, 4000 strong, formed by the Desiderio hill. A Texian sentinel on the church, between Main and Military Plazas, reported a force in view. A man went up. The sentinel said the force had been moved. A spirited altercation ensued. The report of the sentinel caused excitement. In order to arrive at the truth Colonel Travis directed Dr. John Sutherland and Mr. J. W. Smith to ride out and see. They proceeded to Desiderio hill, looked below, and saw an army drawn up, not far from them. They retreated rapidly. Sutherland's horse moved badly. His feet seemed clogged with mud. He turned over, topsy-turvy, fell on Sutherland, crippled him and broke his gun. He laid on Sutherland till Smith alighted, and pulled him off. When they reached the public square the Texians were retiring to the Alamo. On their march they came upon a herd of cattle, twenty-five or thirty in number. These they drove into the Alamo.

Dr. Sutherland wrote an account of the fall of the Alamo. It is the nearest evidence of one of the noble defenders of the Alamo we have. The wounds he received from the fall of his horse rendered him incapable of bearing arms. He was employed in the effort to procure reinforcements to the garrison of the Alamo. This will be noticed hereafter. According to Dr. Sutherland General Santa Anna sent a couple of officers, under a white flag. They were met by Major Morris and Captain Martin, at a foot-bridge on the river, about where Commerce street crosses the San Antonio river. The Mexican officers demanded an uncon ditional surrender, which was refused. As an answer, Colonel Travis ordered a cannon to be fired at the part of town occupied by the Mexican troops.

As stated by Sergeant Becerra, Gen. Santa Anna intended to cross the river below town, out of reach of the fire of the Texian artillery. To obtain wood for the construction of a bridge, he directed Gen. Castrillon to proceed with two companies of the Matamoros battalion to the neighborhood of the Alamo, and take wood from the houses. Gen. Castrillon endeavored to obey the order. He reached the designated point, and was soon under the fire of the Texians. In a short while Castrillon reported to Santa Anna, saying in substance : " If you wish any of the two compa- nies of the battalion to remain alive you had better order them to retire at once." They were withdrawn. Within a few minutes they had lost thirty men. Gen. Castrillon reported having met two ladies. The result of the annunciation was the performance of a mock marriage ceremony—Gen. Santa Anna as groom. and a beautiful Mexican woman as bride, and a rascally Mexican soldier as priest.

Becerra states : " Col. Mora was ordered to take position north and east of the Alamo to prevent escape from the fort."—"A small fort was commenced above the Alamo." This was finished, but was not approved by Gen. Santa Anna. Another fort was constructed by Gen. Amador, nearer the Alamo, on the hill to the northeast. The firing from the Alamo was kept up with spirit.

The intention of Gen. Santa Anna was to take the Alamo by escalade He brought 4,000 troops to Texas. He awaited the arrival of Gen. Tolsa, in command of 2,000 troops. He arrived on the 3d day of March. The exultation and shouts of the Mexi- cans on that day induced Dr. Sutherland to believe that Santa Anna came on that date.

Here the Doctor's estimate of the Texian force will be given:

"The strength of the Texians at Bexar now consisted of one hundred and fifty-two men. Eighty of these were a part of the original garrison, who had not caught the Matamoros fever; twenty-five had returned with Col. Bowie from Goliad. Colonel Travis had brought with him about twenty; Colonel Crockett twelve; Captain Patten eleven. These detachments, with their respective commanders, make the number. A few days after their concentration, some twenty Mexicans of the city joined them, increasing the number to one hundred and seventy two."

Counting the commanders of these bodies and the twenty Mexicans increases the number to 192. The idea suggesting itself to any sensible man would be, what did Gen Santa Anna wáit for Gen. Tolsa for? He had 4,000 men. Was he doubtful of attacking less than 200 men? An expressive compliment to the bravery of the soldiers of Texas. Texas had not paid them. They had not been supplied with medicine, until Dr. Sutherland had been been appointed surgeon. They had nothing to eat but beef and corn bread. These supplies were obtained by accident, as has been seen. There was a spirit in these men that no earthly power could conquer. Death could visit the body. The heroic resolution passed hence with the soul to another world, unchanged and unchangeable. The love of liberty, the determination to maintain it, is a gift from God. In the garrison of the Alamo it ruled.

On the 24th of February Colonel Travis wrote an appeal to the people of Texas:

"COMMANDANCY OF THE ALAMO, Bexar, February 24, 1836.

"Fellow-Citizens and Compatriots: I am beseiged by a thousand or more of the Mexicans under Santa Anna. I have sustained a continued bombardment for twenty-four hours, and have not lost a man. The enemy have demanded a surrender at discretion; otherwise, the garrison is to be put to the sword if the place is taken. I have answered the summons with a cannon shot, and our flag still waves proudly from the walls. *I shall never surrender or retreat.* Then I call on you in the name of liberty, of patriotism, and of everything dear to the American character, to come to our aid with all dispatch. The enemy are receiving reinforcements daily, and will no doubt increase to three or four thousand in four or five days. Though this call may be neglected, I am determined to sustain myself as long as possible, and die like a soldier who forgets not what is due to his own honor and that of his country. Victory or death !

              " W. BARRET TRAVIS,
              "*Lieutenant-Colonel Cowmanding.*"

" P. S.—The Lord is on our side. When the enemy appeared in sight, we had not three bushels of corn. We have since found in deserted houses eighty or ninety bushels, and got into the walls twenty or thirty head of beeves.   " T. "

Col. Travis was unapprised of Santa Anna's number of soldiers. He spoke of what he had seen. Why was his appeal not answered by the appearance of reinforcements? The reason is obvious— the trouble between the Governor and the committee raised to assist him. This committee had forwarded the forces of Texas to Goliad and San Patricio. They had as far as they could super- seded Gen. Houston as commander-in-chief. At the same time they had named no one to take his place. Col. Fannin and Col. Johnson each expected to be commandant of the army to invade Mexico. Had they united their forces they could have defeated the force under Gen. Urrea. He defeated them in detail. Gov. Smith, to whom Gen. Houston remained faithful, after his trouble with the committee, granted the General a furlough till March 1st. The people of Texas were uncertain what they should do. They did little during the period, and the Alamo fell.

Col. Travis wrote to Col. Fannin, February 23d, asking him to come to his relief. Fannin failed from want of transportation. Gen. Santa Anna was notified of Fannin's effort to reinforce Travis. On the 29th of February he dispatched Gen. Sesma, with a force, to meet Fannin. The return of Fannin to Goliad prevented his meeting Gen. Sesma.

Dr. Sutherland and John W. Smith were sent to procure rein- forcements for Col. Travis. They visited Gonzales. There they obtained thirty-two recruits. These they conducted to the neigh- borhood of San Antonio. Smith conducted them to the Alamo, March 1st. Sutherland, still unable to perform military service, remained outside.

The fight continued without abatement. On the 3d of March Col. Travis made his last appeal for help to the President of the Convention, which convened at Washington on the 1st of the month. Among expressions used were the following : " The blood-red banners which waved on the Church at Bexar, and the

MISSION SAN JOSE

camp above him, were tokens that the war was one of vengeance against rebels." To a friend in Washington he wrote ; "Take care of my little boy. If the country should be saved, I may make him a splendid fortune ; but if the country should be lost, and I perish, he will have nothing but the proud recollection that he is the son of a man who died for his country."

William Corner wrote a history of San Antonio in which is published Sidney Lanier's Historical Sketch. He notices the withdrawal of the Mexican troops from the Alamo, March 3d. The following is given as incidents of that day.

"About two hours before sunset on the 3rd of March, 1836, the bombardment suddenly ceased, and the enemy withdrew an unusual distance. * * * Colonel Travis collected all his effective men in a single file, and taking his position in front of the centre, he stood for some moments apparently speechless from emotion; then nerving himself for the occasion, he addressed them substantially as follows:

" 'My companions: Stern necessity compels me to employ the few moments afforded by this probably brief cessation of conflict, in making known the most interesting, yet the most solemn, melancholy and yet unwelcome fact that humanity can realize. * * * Our fate is sealed. Within a few days, perhaps a very few hours, we must be in eternity ! I have deceived you long by the promise of help; but I crave your pardon, hoping that after hearing my explanation you will not only regard my conduct as pardonable, but heartily sympathize with me in my extreme necessity. * * * I have continually received the strongest assurances of help from home. Every letter from the council, and every one that I have seen from individuals at home, have teemed with assurances that our people were willing, ready and anxious to come to our relief. * * * These assurances I received as facts. * * * In the honest and simple confidence of my heart I have transmitted you these promises of help and my confident hope of success. But the promised help has not come, and our hopes are not to be realized. I have evidently confided too much in the promises of our friends; but let us not be in haste to censure them. * * * Our friends were evidently not informed of our perilous condition in time to save us. Doubtless they would have been here by the time they expected any considerable force of the enemy.

" 'My calls on Colonel Fannin remain unanswered, and my messengers have not returned. The probabilities are that his whole command has fallen into the hands of the enemy, or been cut to pieces, and that our couriers have been cut off.' [So does this brave and simple soul refuse to feel any bitterness in the hour of death.] 'Then we must die. * * * Our business is not to make fruitless effort to save our lives, but to choose the manner of our death. But three modes are presented to us; let us choose that by which we may best serve our country. Shall we surrender, and be deliberately shot without taking the life of a single enemy? Shall we try to cut our way out through the Mexican ranks, and be butchered before we can kill twenty of our adversaries? I am opposed to either method. * * ʴ Let us resolve to withstand our enemies to the last, and at each advance to kill as many of them as possible. And when at last they shall storm our fortress, let us kill them as they come ! Kill them as they scale our walls ! Kill them as they leap within ! Kill them as they raise their weapons, and as they use them ! Kill them as they kill our companions ! and continue to kill them as long as one of us shall remain alive ! * * * But I leave every man to his own choice. Should any man prefer to surrender * * * or attempt an escape * * * he is at liberty to do so. My own choice is to stay in the fort and die for my country, fighting as long as breath shall remain in my body. This will I do even if you leave me alone. Do as you think best; but no man can die with me without affording me comfort in the hour of death.'

" Col. Travis then drew his sword, and with the point traced a line upon the ground extending from the right to the left of the file. Then resuming his positioɪ in front of the centre, he said ' I now want every man who is determined to stay here and die with me to come across this line. Who will be the first ? March !' The first respoudent was Tapley Holland, who leaped the line at a bound, exclaiming, ' I am ready to die for my country-' His example was instantly followed by every man in the file, with exception of Rose ———. Every sick man that could walk, arose from his bunk, and tottered across the line. Col. Bowie, who could not leave his bed, said . ' Boys, I am not able to come to you, but I wish some of you would be so kind as to move my cot over there.' Four men instantly ran to the cot, and each lifting a corner carried it over. Then every sick man that could not walk made the same request, and had his bunk moved in the same way.

"Rose was deeply affected, but differently from his companions. He stood till every man but himself had crossed the line. He sank upon the ground, covered his face, and yielded to his own reflections. * * * A bright idea came to his relief; he spoke the Mexican dialect very fluently, and could he once get out of the fort, he might easily pass for a Mexican and effect his escape. He directed a searching glance at rhe cot of Col. Bowie. Col. David Crockett was leaniug over the cot, conversing with its occupant in an undertone. After a few seconds Bowie looked at Rose and said : ' You seem not to be willlng to die with us, Rose.' ' No, said Rose, ' I am not prepared to die, and shall not do so if I can avoid it.' Then Crockett also looked at him, and said : ' You may as well conclude to die with us, old man, for escape is impossible.' Rose made no reply, but looked at the top of the wall. ' I have often done worse than climb that wall,' thought he. Suiting the action to the thought, ne sprang up, seized his wallet of unwashed clothes, and ascended the wall. Standing on its top, he looked down within to take a last view of his dying friends. They were now all in motion, but what they were doing he heeded not ; overpowered by his feelings, he looked away, and saw them no more. * * * He threw down his wallet, and leaped after it. * * * He took the road which led down the river, around a bend to the ford, and through the town by the church. He waded the river at the ford, and passed through the town. He saw no person, * * * but the doors were all closed, and San Antonio appeared as a deserted city

" After passing through the town, he turned down the river. A stillness as of death prevailed. When he had gone about a quarter of a mile below the town, his ears were saluted by the thunder of the bombardment, which was then renewed. That thunder continued to remind him that his friends were true to their cause, by a continued roar, with but slight intervals, until a little before sunrise on the morning of the 6th, when it ceased, and he heard it no more."

Rose stopped at the house of Zuber. His account of the incidents of March 3d was published in the Texas Almanac of 1873. Mr. W. P. and Mary Ann Zuber are responsible for its anthenticity as coming from Rose.   They affirm that Rose proceeded to Nacogdoches county.

After the arrival of Gen. Tolza there was, as previously stated, a suspension of operations for a time.   The intentions of Gen. Santa Anna seems to have been to allow no cessation of attack, and to allow the small garrison of Texians no time to sleep.   They were overworked, worn down, almost asleep when firing.

Sergeant Becerra thus describes the preparations for a final assault : " *On* the 3d of March Gen. Tolza arrived.   The great est activity prevailed in every department.   The plan of assault was formed and communicated to the commanders of corps, and others, on the 5th.   On the same day ammunition, scaling ladders, etc., were distributed.   Everything was made ready for the storming.   During the night troops were placed in position   About three o'clock on the morning of the 6th the battalion Matamoros was marched to a point near the river, and above the Alamo.   In their rear were two thousand men under Gen. Cos.   Gen. Castrillon commanded this part of the army.   Gen. Tolza's command held the ground below the Alamo.   Gen. Santa Anna spent the night in the work near the Alamo.   The troops were to march to the attack when the bugler at headquarters sounded the advance. * * *   The bugle was sounded at 4 o'clock a. m., March 6, 1836.

" The troops of Gen. Castrillon moved in silence.   They reached the fort, planted scaling ladders, and commenced ascending, some mounted on the shoulders of others.   A terrible fire belched from the interior.   Men fell from the scaling ladders by the score, many pierced through the head by balls, others felled by clubbed guns. The dead and wounded covered the ground.   After half an hour of fierce conflict, after the sacrifice of many lives, the column of Gen. Castrillon succeeded in making a lodgment in the upper part of the Alamo to the northeast.   It was a sort of outwork.   I think it is now used as a lot or courtyard.   This seeming advantage was a mere prelude to the desperate struggle which ensued. The doors of the Alamo building were barricaded by bags of sand as high as the neck of a man ; the windows also.   On the top of the roofs of the different apartments were rows of sand bags to cover the beseiged.

" *Our* troops, inspired by success, continued the attack with energy and boldness.   The Texians fought like devils.   It was at short range—muzzle to muzzle, hand to hand, musket and rifle, bayonet and bowie knife—all were mingled in confusion. Here a squad of Mexicans, there a Texian or two. The crash of firearms, the shouts of defiance, the cries of the dying and wounded, made a din almost infernal. The Texians defended desperately every inch of the fort—overpowered by numbers, they would be forced to abandon a room. They would rally in the next, and defend it until further resistance became impossible.

"Gen. Tolza's command forced an entrance at the door of the church building. He met the same determined resistance without and within. He won by force of numbers and a great sacrifice of life.

"There was a long room on the ground floor. It was darkened. Here the fight was bloody. It proved to be the hospital. A detachment of which I had command had captured a piece of artillery. It was placed near the door of the hospital, doubly charged with grape and canister, and fired twice. We entered and found the corpses of fifteen Texians. On the outside we afterward found forty-two dead Mexicans.

"On the top of the church building I saw eleven Texians They had some small pieces of artillery and were firing on the cavalry and on those engaged in making the escalade. Their ammunition was exhausted, and they were loading with pieces os iron and nails. The captured piece was placed in a position to reach them, doubly charged, and fired with so much effect that they ceased working their pieces."

Sergeant Becerra was of opinion that the last two men killed were Travis and Col. Crockett, though he admitted he did not know them personally, and might be mistaken as to their identity.

"The Alamo, as has been stated, was entered at daylight; the fight did not cease 'till 9 o'clock. * * *

"Gen. Santa Anna directed Col. Mora to send out his cavalry to bring in wood. This was done. The bodies of the heroic Texians were burned. Their remains became offensive. They were afterward collected and buried by Col. Juan N. Seguin.

Sergeant Becerra said

"There was an order to gather our own dead and wounded. It was a fearful sight. Our lifeless soldiers covered the ground surrounding the Alamo. They were heaped inside the fortress. Blood and brains covered the earth and floors, and had spattered the walls. The ghastly faces of our comrades met our gaze, and we removed them with despondent hearts.   Our loss in front of the Alamo was represented at two thousand killed, and more than three hundred wounded.   The killed were generally struck on the head.   The wounds were in the neck, or shoulder, seldom below that.   The firing of the besieged was fearfully precise. When a Texas rifle was leveled on a Mexican he was considered as good as dead.   All this indicates the dauntless bravery and the cool self-possession of the men who were engaged in a hopeless conflict with an enemy numbering more than twenty to one. They inflicted on us a loss ten times greater than they sustained. The victory of the Alamo was dearly bought.   Indeed, the price in the end was well-nigh the ruin of Mexico.''

The number of Texas dead at the Alamo was never accurately ascertained.   It included the whole number of the volunteers beseiged.   The number of Mexicans taking service with the Texians was stated at twenty or twenty-five.   These were, many of them, sent out on various occasions by Col. Travis.   When divested of their arms, it was no difficult matter to pass the Mexican on guard without much scrutiny.   Mrs. Candelaria, Colonel Bowie's nurse, gives the names of four Mexican's who were alive when the Alamo fell, or were killed fighting.   Mrs. Alsbury, in her statement, mentions the killing of one Mexican after the Mexicans entered the Alamo.   The Texians lost in the siege is not positively known.   It was certainly less than two hundred.

Dr. Sutherland endeavored to learn the exact loss of the Mexicans at San Antonio.   He says:

'' The messenger who was sent by the Navarro family, at San Antonio, to Colonel Seguin, at Gonzales, four days after the fall, reported the enemy's loss to have been about fifteen hundred.'' Dr. Sutherland visited Gen. Santa Anna after he was made prisoner at San Jacinto.   He questioned Gen. Santa Anna's private secretary as to the number of men in the army at San Antonio, and the number killed in the operations.   His reply, as stated by Dr. Sutherland, was, '' we brought to San Antonio five thousand men, and lost during the siege fifteen hundred and forty-four of the best of them.   The Texians fought more like devil's than men.''   Santa Anna and Almonte were both present at the time, and, if the statement had deviated far from the truth, for it certainly derogated from their soldierly (qualifications) for them to have denied it, without scrupling to question the veracty of their fellow (prisoner.) That answer was, no doubt, made by Ramon Martinez Coro, who signed the order for the attack on the Alamo March 6th. The gentleman acting as interpreter was Captain Patten. Gen. Santa Anna and Col. Almonte were both present, and neither of them denied the allegation. Almonte was edu cated in the United States, and spoke English fluently.

Dr. Sutherland observes · "Ruiz says it was estimated at 1,600," speaking of the Mexican loss. Again, speaking of one charge made by the Toluca battalion, he says: "They commenced to scale the walls and suffered severely. Out of 8oo men 130 only were left alive." Dr. Sutherland argues that 670 were killed out of 800 men ; 1,600 slain in all would be no exaggeration. The writer came to Texas in 1836. There were then in San Augustine county Mexicans who were made prisoners at San Jacinto. They represented the Mexican loss at the Alamo at 2,500. They may have meant the killed and wounded.

Before referring to matters pertaining to Texians, the order of General Santa Anna to attack the Alamo, by sealing the walls, will be given. It may show that Sergeant Becerra's memory was defective in some particulars, but is more a corroboration of his version than a denial.

"GENERAL ORDERS."

[For the private information of Generals of Division and Corps Commanders.]

"As it becomes necessary to make a decisive movement against the enemy defending the fortress of the Alamo, His Excellency, the General-in-Chief, directs that by four o'clock on to-morrow morning the attacking columns shall be stationed within gunshot of their first line of intrenchments, for the purpose of making the assault, upon the signal to be given by His Excellency, which will be the sounding of the bugle from the north battery.

"The first column will be commanded by General Don Martin Perfecto de Cos, and in his default, by me, (the Commander-in-Chief). This column will be composed of the Aldamas battalion of regulars, with the exception of the company of Grenadiers, and the three first companies of the volunteer battalion of San Luis.

"The second column will be commanded by General Don Francisco Duque, and in his default, by General Don Manuel Fernando Castrillon. This column will be composed of the three remaining companies of the San Luis battalion of volunteers.

"The third column will be commanded by Colonel Don Jose Maria Romero, and in his default, by Colonel Don Mariano Salas. This column will be composed of the infantry companies, in full force, of the Matamoros and Jimenes battalions of regulars.

"The fourth column will be commanded by Colonel Don Juan Morelos, and in his default, by Colonel Don Jose Minon. This column will be composed of the cavalry companies of the Matamoros and Jimenes battalions of regulars, and the San Luis battalion of volunteers.

"The General-in-Chief will, at the proper time, designate the points against which the attacking columns will operate, at which time commanding officers will also receive their orders.

"The reserve will be composed of the battalion of Sappers and Miners, and the five companies of the Grenadiers of the Matamoros, Jimenes and Aldamas battalions of regulars, and of the Toluca and San Luis battalions of volunteers.

"The reserve will be commanded by the General-in-Chief in person, at the time of making the attack, but these forces will be organized by Colonel Don Agustin Amat, under whose control they will remain from this evening, and who will conduct them to the point which will be designated to him at the proper time.

"The first column will be provided with ten scaling ladders, two crow bars and two axes; the second will be provided with the same quantity; the third with six, and the fourth with two. The men carrying the ladders will sling their guns over their shoulders, so as to leave them entirely free to place their ladders wherever they may be directed.

"Grenadier and cavalry companies will be supplied with six packages of cartridges to the man, and to the infantry companies four with two extra flints. The latter will be encumbered with neither overcoats, blankets nor anything which will impede the rapidity of their movements. During the day all caps will be provided with chin straps. Corps commanders will pay particular attention to this provision, and are also required to see that the men are provided with shoes, or other covering for their feet.

"The men composing the attacking column will retire to rest at sundown, preparatory to moving at midnight.

"The men not well drilled will remain at their quarters.

SCENE NEAR MILL BRIDGE, SAN ANTONIO.

"Arms, particularly bayonets, will be put in the best condition.

"When the moon rises the riflemen of the San Luis battalion of volunteers will retire to their quarter, abandoning the points they cover along the line, so as to give them time to put their equipage in readiness.

"The cavalry, under the command of General Don Joaquin Ramirezy y Sesma, will occupy the Alameda, and saddle up at 3 o'clock in the morning. It will be their duty to watch the camp, and prevent the escape of anyone who may attempt to do so.

"The honor of the nation, and of the army, being involved in this contest against the daring foreigners in our front, His Excelleney, the General-in-Chief, expects that each man will perform his duty, and contribute his share in securing a day of glory to his country, and of honor to the Federal Government, which knows how to honor the brave men of the army of operations who shall distinguish themselves by performing feats of valor.

JUAN VALENTINE AMADOR."

"I certify the foregoing to be a true copy.

"RAMON MARTINES CORO, Secretary."

"A correct translation.   DAVID G. WHITING.

"Translator General Land Office."

N. B.—This order, Becerra said, was issued March 5, 1836, and copied next day.

This was the order given by the President of Mexico, and commander of her armies, to six thousand Mexicans, the elite of the Mexican army, who had been besieging less than two hundred Texians for thirteen days. It speaks for itself.

On March 7th General Santa Anna issued a " Proclamation," in which he speaks of the immolation of the Texians as a matter of justice, and argues that the "Army of *O*perations" has been marched into Texas for the performance of such deeds.

REMARKS.

Colonel Bowie had been ordered by General Houston to proceed to Goliad and adjacent points, and confer with officers in command. General Houston's intention were to withdraw the Texian forces from advanced positions and concentrate them, with the object of meeting and defeating the Mexican army of invasion which was believed to be advancing upon Texas. After the performance of that duty he proceeded to San Antonio, where he resided. On the 11th or 12th of February, 1836, Colonel Neill left San Antonio, accompanied by Deaf Smith. William Barrett Travis, Lieutenant Colonel of the regular army of Texas, was deputed to the command. The volunteers on dnty at San Antonio objected to be commanded by a regular officer. Colonel Travis, with a sincere desire to promote the public good, ordered an election. Colonel Bowie was the choice of the men.

On February 14th a general report was made to Governor Smith, which concludes as follows: " By an understanding of to-day, Col. J. Bowie has command of the volunteers and Col. W. B. Travis of tbe regulars and volunteer cavalry. All general orders and correspondence will be, henceforth, signed by both until Col. Neill's return.   JAMES BOWIE,

" W. BARRETT TRAVIS,   Commander of Volunteers."

     " Commander of Cavalry."

[Col, Seth Shephard's oration on the " Fall of the Alamo," San Marcos, July 8th,, 1889.]

James Butler Bonham had been a schoolmate of Col. Travis ; he was one of the messengers sent to Col. Fannin by Col. Travis asking for help. After the performance of that duty he delayed returning to the Alamo until March 3d. According to Hon. Seth Shephard, Bonham declined to remain outside San Antonio. He affirmed : ": I will report the result ot mv mission to Travis, or die in the attempt." " Mounted on a cream-colored horse, with a white handkerchief floating from his hat—a signal previously arranged with Travis—he dashed through the Mexican lines amid a shower of bullets, and entered unharmed the gates which were thrown open to receive him. Unable to save his comrades, he was determined to die with them.''

Col. Bowie fell sick in the early part of the siege. Mrs. Candelaria was his attendant. He died with unfaltering courage. A Mexican gentleman told Mrs. Sam Maverick that his body was hoisted on Mexican bayonets until a Mexican officer ordered them to desist.

Mrs. Dr. Alsbury and her little sister were in the Alamo when it fell. A Mexican defender of the Alamo was bayonetted while clinging to her for help, and to avoid death. She was carried off by the brother of her first husband. Her son, then small, is yet in San Antonio.

Mrs. Dickinson was allowed to leave the town. Her young child, afterwards styled " The Daughter of the Alamo," was her companion. They are both dead.

Dr. Sutherland tells us something of Col. Crockett: " Colonel David Crockett arrived, * * * with twelve others, direct from Tennessee. Crockett was immediately offered a command by Col. Travis, and called upon by the crowd for a speech. The former honor he would not accept ; but mounted a goods-box on the civil plaza, amid prolonged cheers of the people. The applause, however, was followed by profound silence, when the full-toned voice of the distinguished speaker rose gradually above the audience and fell smooth and lively upon the ears of all ; its sound was familiar to many who had heard it in days past, while the hearts of all beat a lively response to the patriotic sentiments which fell from his lips. Eloquent applause greeted him, as he related in his own peculiar style, some of those jolly anecdotes with which he often regaled his friends, and which he only could tell with appropriate grace. He alluded frequently to his past career, and during the course of his remarks stated that not long since he had been a candidate for Congress in his native district, and that during the canvass he told his constituents that 'if they did not elect him, they might all go to h——, and he would go to Texas.' After which he concluded, in substance, as follows : 'And fellow-citizens, I am among you. I have come to your country, though I hope, not with any selfish motive whatever. I have come to aid you all that I can in your noble cause. I shall identify myself with your interests, and all the honor that I desire is that of defending as a high private, in common with my fellow-citizens, the liberties of our common country.' "

As long as liberty has a follower the names of Crockett and the other defenders of the Alamo will have an admirer. Their unselfish and undaunted heroism confers upon them the immortal remembrance of the lovers of freedom. The affair of the Alamo caused intense excitement in the United States, in fact, throughout the civilized world. An Englishman, named Nagle, had the honor of originating the "Monument Erected to the heroes of the Alamo." It stood at the entrance of the Capitol at Austin. This building was burned in 1880, and the monument suffered injury. On the top of each front were the names of Travis, Bowie, Crockett and Bonham. The inscription on the north front was: "To The God Of The Fearless And The Free Is Dedicated This Altar Of The ALAMO." On the west front: "Blood of Heroes Hath Stained me. Let The Stones of The ALAMO Speak, That Their IMMOLATION Be Not FORGOTTEN." On the south front: "Be They Enrolled With Leonidas In The Host Of The Mighty Dead." On the east front: "Thermopylæ Had Her Messenger of Defeat, But The ALAMO Had NONE."

Mrs. Maverick and Mrs. Canterbury, at that time Mrs. Wilson I. Riddle, both were acquainted with Mr. Nagle, and speak kindly of him. He received from the Legislature of Texas a small consideration for the monument, and is since dead. His memory should be honored by every friend of Texas.

Sergeant Becerra was made a prisoner at San Jacinto. In the war between Mexico and the United States he was in the service of the latter. When he died he was a Mexican veteran of the United States.

Colonel Travis' son was a member of the Legislature of Texas. He was a captain in the regular army of the United States, and belonged to the regiment commanded by Col. Sydney Johnson. He had a daughter also. She was living some years ago.

After the fall of the Alamo there were thirty-three wives left widows in Gonzales.

Mr. J. W. Smith was highly respected by the Texians. He died while a member of Congress at Washington, on the Brazos river. He is worthy of consideration as one of the tried and true friends of Texas in her days of peril.

Dr. Sutherland lived many years after the revolution of 1836.

He was honored by all as one of the able and trusted men who served his couutry with zeal and fidelity when her cause appeared almost hopeless. He died full of years and full of honors.

Mrs. Candelaria is till living. She claims to be over one hundred yeats of ag:. The State of Texas has granted her a pension.

However, want of space prevents the mention of many who performed important services to Texas in the days of trial and adversity.

Captain Reuben M. Potter, U. S. A., retired, was an efficient friend of the Republic of Texas. In the days of gloom he wrote the " Hymn of the Alamo," and predicted the success of her cause, which is herewith presented ·

"Rise ! man the wall—our clarion's blast
   Now sounds its final reveille—
This dawning morn must be the last
   Our fated band shall ever see.
To life, but not to hope, farewell ;
   Your trumpet's clang, and cannon's peal,
And storming shout, ar d clash of steel
   Is ours, but not our country's knell.
Welcome the Spartan's death—
   'Tis no despairing strife—
We fall—we die—but our expiring breath
   Is freedom's breath of life.

" 'Here on this new Thermopylæ
   Our monument shall tower on high,
And 'Alamo' hereafter be
   On bloodier fields the battle cry.'
Thus Travis from the rampart cried,
   And when his warriors saw the foe
Like whelming billows move below,
   At once each dauntless heart replied ·
'Welcome the Spartan's death—
   'Tis no despairing strife—
We fall—we die—but our expiring breath
   Is freedom's breath of life.

"They come—like autumn leaves they fall
   Yet hordes on hordes they onward rush ;
With gory tramp they mount the wall
   Till numbers the defenders crush.
The last was felled—the fight to gain—
   Well may the ruffians quake to tell
How Travis and his hundred fell
   Amid a thousand foemen slain.
They died 'he Spartan's death,
   But not in hopeless strife ;
Like brothers died—and their expiring breath
   Was freedom's breath of life.

The convention of Texas met at Washington, on the Brazos, March 1, 1836. On the second day of that month they issued a declaration of independence. They formed a constitution, elected David G. Burnet provisional president, Lorenzo de Zavala vice-president. They also pronounced Sam Houston general-in-chief of the Texas army. President Burnet appointed the following gentlemen as his cabinet ·

SAMUEL P. CARSON....................................Secretary of State
BAILEY HARDEMAN................. ......Secretary of the Treasury
THOMAS J. RUSK........ ....Secretary of War
ROBERT POTTER........... .... Secretary of the Navy
DAVID THOMAS ....Attorney General

They adjourned, and many of the members proceeded at once to the Texas army

On the 21st day of April, 1836, the battle of San Jacinto was fought. General Lopez de Santa Anna, president of Mexico, and commander-in-chief of her army, was made a prisoner of war. He recognized the independence of Texas. The balance of the Mexican army, in accordance with its stipulations, was permitted to march out of Texas unmolested. Mexico received the benefits of the treaty, and according to the laws of nations could not go back on that agreement, inuring to her benefit. Texas became sovereign, free and independent by reason of that treaty.

SAN ANTONIO EVENTS.

In the papers preserved at San Antonio is an account of a visit to the place of LaFitte, the celebrated pirate. He was placed in confinement, and afterwards liberated. General X. B. Debray translated the document. The General published the account several years since.

Below are given some notices of events without regard to the date.

During the contest of the Mexican revolution, there were operations near San Antonio. In 1812, Lieut. Magee, late of the United States army, conveyed a force into Texas. He assumed the rank of colonel. He captured La Bahia-Goliad. He died there. Major Kemper succeeded him. He marched to San Antonio at the head of 1500 men. Gen. Salcedo, with a force of 2500 men, met him on the Salado, about nine miles from town, where a fight occurred. The Americans were successful, losing only a few men. The Imperials lost more than 1000, with all their camp equipage. This engagement occurred about March

28, 1813. The next day Col. Kemper entered San Antonio. Fourteen officers of rank were made prisoners. Gen. Bernardo, who was ostensibly in command of the revolutionists, now assumed more authority. He ordered Capt. Delgado to escort these officers to the coast, where it was pretended a vessel lay, where they were to embark for New Orleans. Delgado proceeded a few miles from the city, where he massacred these officers in cold blood. This criminal act was the cause of profound disapproval by the Americans. Colonel Kemper and Major Ross resigned and left Texas. It was ascertained that Gen. Bernardo had authorized Capt. Delgado to commit the barbarous tragedy, and he was relieved from command.

Captain Perry assnmed command of the Americans. General Elizondo, who betrayed Hidalgo to the Spaniards, entered Texas with about 3000 men. He moved to the vicinity of San Antonio, dispersed and killed many of the guard in charge of the American horses, yet failed to enter the city. Elizondo encamped on the Alazan creek, and had erected two bastions. The Americans decided on a plan of battle. On the night of October 4, 1815, they marched out of town and attacked the Royalists early in the mornıng while prayers were being said. After several hours of hard fighting the Spaniards fled, having lost a thousand in killed, wounded and prisoners; American loss, forty-seven killed and the same number wounded, most of whom died.

Just after this affair General Toledo, a Cuban, arrived and took command. He organized a governing junta, appointed civil officers and restored the reign of law and order.

Gen. Elizondo retreated in the direction of the Rio Grande. Gen. Arredondo was commandant of that section. He united his forces with those of Elizondo and set out for San Antonio. South of the Medina river he threw up a breastwork in the form of a capital A, the open part facing San Antonio. In advance of this he placed some men. The republicans came—attacked the advance. They charged the advance, pursued them into the forks of the work, where the Spaniards opened a terrific fire upon them from each side of their works. Gen. Toledo had unfortunately placed the Americans upon the right and left wings of his army. After discovering the trap he had entered, Gen. Toledo ordered a retreat. The American left wing obeyed. but the right wing refused, saying "they never retreated." These men continued to fight. "They performed progidies of valor." In the unequal contest nearly all of them were killed. The retreating column was pursued by the Spanish cavalry, and many of them were butchered. The retreat was continued across Texas. Seventy or eighty republicans surrendered at Spanish Bluff, on Trinity river. They were inhumanly butchered. "Only ninety-three Americans succeeded in reaching Nacogdoches." This was the end of the American campaign in Texas in 1812 and 1813. Arredondo treated the people of Bexar with much cruelty—tried to confiscate property, forced ladies to cook for soldiers, and mistreated men.

An American, George Antonio Nixon, who came to San Antonio at an early day, affirmed that the day he arrived a swarm of bees settled on the Catholic church in the Main Plaza. He said many Mexicans asserted that the North Americans would soon follow the bees. He seemed to believe that the Mexicans of this section generally entertained that opinion. He died in San Augustine many years ago.

During 1819 General Long entered Texas. He established a provisional government at Nacogdoches—declared Texas an independent republic. He sought LaFitte's assistance, and failed to obtain it. He eventually conducted an expedition to La Bahia, which he captured. From this period his history is problematical. He was carried to the City of Mexico where he was assassinated. His wife remained at Point Bolivar many months awaiting his return. The morning and evening guns were fired with regularity. Eventually her friends informed her of the General's fate, and relieved her. She was a lady of fine accomplishments and great bravery.

In 1831, Colonel Bowie, in charge of nine men and two servants, formed a party to visit a silver mine near the head of San Saba river. While on the way they were informed by Isaonie, a chief of the Comanches, that a large party of Wacoes and Two-wokanas were following them, determined to take their scalps. The Americans moved on. They had arrived within a few miles of the San Saba river. They were preparing to break camp when they were saluted by the war whoop by one hundred and sixty-four Indians. Arrangements were promptly made for defense. A terrific resistance was made. Many Indians were killed. They fired the grass, but with no good effect. During the burning of

SAN ANTONIO IN 1853.

the grass they removed their dead. That night they cried over their dead. The next morning they carried them to a cave a mile off. They then left. Their loss was reported to be eighty-one killed and wounded ; American loss, one man killed, three wounded ; one horse killed, three wounded.

They remained in camp about eight days, taking care of the wounded, then marched slowly for home. Mr. Hamm, one of the party, over eighty years of age, described the fight to the writer. They reached San Antonio after nightfall. The people had concluded they had been killed. When it was ascertained that Col. Bowie and party had returned, the people were rejoiced. They illuminated the place and did all they could to welcome the visitors.

Gen. Sam Houston came to Texas in 1832. He was advised to come by Gen. Andrew Jackson. He appears to have had authority as an agent to the Cherokee and other United States Indians.

In February, 1840, the Comanche Indians were requested to meet the Texas Secretary of War, Gen. A. S. Johnson and others at San Antonio. They agreed to bring with them thirteen white captives. They came, and brought but one, Miss Lockhart. She told they had others in their camps. The Americans very candidly told the Comanche chiefs they would have to bring in the other prisoners, comply with their words, before they could or would be liberated. The Comanches seemed to talk with bravado and defiantly. The company of Capt. Tom Howard was marched into the council room. The Comanches were told they would be held as prisoners until the other prisoners were brought in. The Comanches began fighting at once. They wounded Capt. Howard. The fight became general. Thirty-two warriors, three women and two children were killed. Twenty-seven women and children were made prisoners. Texian loss, seven killed and eight wounded. A Comanche woman afterwards braught in six or seven prisoners. This affair was preceded by a long and bloody war.

On August 10, 1840, the battle of Plum Creek was fought; from fifty to eighty Comanches killed. Texians commanded by General Felix Houston. Captain Ben McCulloch deserves great credit for preparing the citizens to attack the Indians. In that engagement a man shot a squaw, and exclaimed: "By jingo! I am thinning them now"

In 1841 Captain John C. Hays began gaining distinction as a successful commander. He was situated near San Antonio, and was the defender of the southern and western frontier. On April 7, 1841, he defeated the Mexicans near Laredo.

March 5, 1842, General Rafael Vazquez sent Colonel Corazco to demand the surrender of San Antonio. The reply was promised the next day by two o'clock, through Mr. Van Ness and Mr. Morris. Meantime, Capt. Hays and company had concluded to retreat upon the Guadalupe. Vasquez came into the city. Considerable private property was taken by private soldiers. A goodly number of Mexican citizens left San Antonio with the invaders. They remained but two days.

April 11, 1842, Gen. Adrian Woll entered San Antonio at the head of 1200 men. Capt. Hays had retired to the Salado, about eight miles distant- Capt. Matthew Caldwell, with eighty men, joined Hays. The latter was sent to San Antonio to entice Gen. Woll to pursue him. Woll advanced with 800 men, and found Caldwell on the creek with 220 men. Woll attacked Caldwell about eleven o'clock. At sundown he retired, sustaining an estimated loss of sixty killed and sixty wounded; Texian loss, one killed and nine wounded. Capt. Dawson, of La Grange, Texas, in command of 53 men, was marching to assist Col. Caldwell. He was attacked by a portion of Gen. Woll's command. He halted his men in a grove of mesquite bushes. The enemy used artillery. Capt. Dawson sent out a white flag. It was disregarded, and fired on. Thirty-two of Dawson's men were killed, fifteen surrendered; many were wantonly butchered after they yielded themselves prisoners of war.

Many men were hurrying to the scene of conflict. Gen. Woll seemed to appreciate the fact. He ordered his baggage to leave for Mexico that night. The command followed the next morning, April 18th. He acquired considerable plunder, and several Mexicans abandoned Texas and went with him.

Gen. Woll made 63 prisoners at San Antonio, many of them men of distinction. Among them were Colonel Sam Maverick, Judge Hutchinson, Major Colquhon, Judge William E. Jones, Wilson I and John Riddle, John Twohig, Pat Morgan, Dr. Booker,

Dr. McKay, John Howard and other gentlemen of respectability and influence.

Colonel Caldwell's force was then increased to about 500 men. His intention was to force Gen, Woll to fight. It was unfortunately the fact that ambitious men desired to command. They converted the expedition into an electioneering hubbub ; let Gen. Woll escape, after Capt. Hays had attacked and captured one of his batteries. Colonel Caldwell had done exceedingly well and merited the command.

"COLT'S SIX - SHOOTERS."

The five-shooters, the invention of Col. Colt, were offered to the public some time before they were recognized and adopted as the best firearm of that class then in existence. Few were sold, and the inventor was losing heart. Mr. Swante Swinson, in early days a merchant in Austin, Texas, and since a banker in the City of New York, was a friend of Col. Colt. He made him a present of two five-shooters. Mr. Swinson had the good sense to discover their value. He was instrumental in procuring their delivery to Capt. Hays. He approved them. The then government of the Republic of Texas procured a supply of the pistols and armed Hays' rangers.

In 1844 Hays had a command of about fourteen men on a small creek, probably thirty miles above San Antonio. He discovered in his neighborhood a command of seventy-five Comanches. They were waiting for an advantage to attack. Hays was too adroit to give them that advantage. They formed on a hill. He galloped around it and attacked them in the rear. The Indians charged them. They formed in a circle and used both rifle and pistol. The Comanches used their lances. They were greatly surprised at the repeating pistols. They moved off, followed by the indomitable rangers. On two occasions the chief induced them to charge again. He was making a third effort when Gillespie shot him. The Indians retreated in wild confusion. Capt. Gillespie was killed in the fight at Monterey. Sam Walker, afterwards a colonel in Mexico, and killed at Huamantla, was wounded also. Many others were slightly hurt. The Comanches suffered a loss of thirty-five. This engagement placed the Colt's five-shooter in general notice and high esteem.

Col. Sam Walker, during the Mexican war, visited Col. Colt.

He was reported to have recommended a larger weapon than the five-shooter. When Col. Hays' regiment reached Vera Cruz, in Mexico, in the fall of 1847, there they found a supply of six-shooters, and his command was armed with them. The soldiers, some of them, were unacquainted with them and suffered some accidents. The writer remembers one man wounding his own foot, another killing his own horse, and so on

JOHN S. FORD, One of the Committee.

In addition to the foregoing, your committee have concluded to add the annexed :

The points occupied by the Mexican forces during the siege of the Alamo, particularly on the morning of March 6, 1836, are of interest. A fort was built northeast of the Alamo, which was situated, probably, on what is now known as Dignowity Hill. This conclusion is strengthened by the fact that in making improvements on that hill cannon balls and other articles of that character were found. These balls may have been thrown from the Alamo. It is probable that the present site of the street, Avenue C, was included by the troops occupying that fort. The cavalry were stationed at the foot of what was then known as Powder House Hill to prevent escapes from the Alamo. That section is now covered by graveyards. The Mexicans moved in four columns when they made the final attack. Of course, they advanced from four different points.

The people and the Legislature have endeavored to honor the memory of the men who were prominently engaged in defense of the country. The capital of the State is named in commemoration of Stephen F. Austin, the father of Texas. The capital of the Republic of Texas in early days was named Houston, in honor of Gen. Sam Houston, the Washington of Texas. Travis, the county in which the present capital is located, was named for the disinterested patriot, who sacrificed his life in the cause of Texas. Bowie, Bonham, in fact nearly all of the heroes of the Alamo, and quite all the men who distinguished themselves in the service of the Republic and the State of Texas have been remembered by a grateful people.

Among these is Col. Juan N. Seguin, who was an officer at San Jacinto, and for whom the town of Seguin is named.

The weight of years, and in many instances, the hand of poverty is laid heavily upon the old patriots who nobly aided Texas in her days of infancy and feebleness. Some of those who suffered, fought and talked for the Lone Star State, yet live in San Antonio We may mention : Mrs. Mary Maverick, Mrs. Elizabeth Canterbury, Mrs. Amanda J. Dignowity, Capt. Nat Mitchell, a former soldier of San Jacinto, William McMasters, veteran of San Jacinto, Gen. H. P. Bee, Col. John S. Ford, Jacob Golls, Mexican veteran, Mr. George Linswiler, Capt. William Edgar, Capt. P. S. Buquor, formerly mayor of San Antonio, and a few others whose names are not remembered.

C. L. DIGNOWITY, Chairman,
H. P. BEE,
WM. H. YOUNG.

A list of the names of those who fell in the Alamo, at San Antonio dé Bexar, 6th March, 1836:

NAME	RANK	WHERE FROM
W. Barrett Travis	Lt.-Colonel	Commandant
James Bowie	"	
J. Washington		Tennessee
—— Forsyth	Captain	New York
—— Harrison	"	Tennessee
William Blazeley	"	Louisiana N. O 'Greys
Wm. C. M. Baker	"	Mississippi
S. B. Evans	"	
W. R. Carey	"	Texas
S C. Blair	"	Texas
—— Gilmore	"	Tennessee
Robert White	"	
John Jones	Lieutenant	N. O. Greys
J. G. Baugh	Lt.-Adjutant	
Robert Evans	Lt.-Mast Ord.	Ireland
—— Williamson	Sergt.-Major	
Charles Despalier	Aid to Travis	
Eliel Melton	Lt.-Quartermaster	
—— Anderson	Asst. "	
—— Burwell	" "	
Dr. Michison	Surgeon	
Dr. Amos Pollard	"	
Dr. Thompson	"	
Green B. Jemison	Ensign	
DaVid Crockett	Private	Tennessee
E. Nelson	"	South Carolina
—— Nelson	"	Texas
Wm. H. Smith	"	Nacogdoches
Lewis Johnson	"	Trinity, Texas
E. P. Mitchell	"	Georgia
F. Desanque	"	Philadelphia, Penn.
—— Thurston	"	Kentucky.
—— Moore		
Christopher Parker	"	Natchez, Miss.
C. Huskell	"	
—— Rose	"	Nacogdoches
John Blair	"	Nacogdoches
David Wilson	"	Nacogdoches
John M. Hays	"	Tennessee
—— Stuart	"	
W. K. Simpson	"	
W. D. Sutherland	"	Navidad, Texas
Dr. W. Howell	"	New Orleans
—— Butler	"	New Orleans
Charles Smith	"	
—— McGregor	"	Scotland
—— Rusk	"	
Charles Hawkins	"	Ireland
Samuel Holloway	"	
—— Brown	"	
C. S. Smith	"	
—— Browne	"	Philadelphia
—— Kedeson	"	
Wm. Wells	"	Tennessee
Wm. Cummings	"	Pennsylvania
—— Voluntine	"	
—— Cockran		
R. W. Valentine	"	
S. Holloway	"	
Isaac White		
—— Day	"	
Robert Muselman	"	New Orleans
Robert Crossman	"	New Orleans
Richard Starr	"	England
J. G. Garrett	"	New Orleans (or Ganett)
James Dimkin	"	England
Robert B. Moore	"	New Orleans
Wm. Linn	"	Boston
—— Hutchinson	"	
Wm. Johnson	"	Philadelphia
E. Nelson	"	
Geo. Tumlinson		

LIST OF NAMES.—*Continued.*

NAME	RANK	WHERE FROM
Wm. Deardorf	Private	
Dan'l Bourne	"	England
—— Ingram	"	England
W I. Lewis	"	Wales,
Charles Zanco	"	Denmark
James Ewing		
Robert Cunningham	"	
S. Burns	"	Ireland
George Neggin		
J. B. Bonham	"	South Carolina
—— Robinson	"	Scotland
Marcus Sewell		(Shoe Maker)
—— Harriss	"	Kentucky
John Flanders		
Isaac Ryan	"	Opelousas
I Jackson	"	Ireland
Almeron Dickinson	Lieutenant	Gonzales
George C. Kimbell	"	Gonzales
James George	Private	Gonzales
Dolphin Floyd	"	Gonzales
Thomas Jackson	"	Gonzales
Jacob Durst	"	Gonzales
George W. Cottle	"	Gonzales
Andrew Kent	"	Gonzales
Thomas R. Miller	"	Gonzales
Isaac Baker	"	Gonzales
William King	"	Gonzales
Jesse McCoy	"	Gonzales
Claiborne Wright	"	Gonzales
William Fishback	"	Gonzales
Isaac Millsaps	"	Gonzales
Galba Fuqua	"	Gonzales
John Davis	"	Gonzales
Albert Martin	"	Gonzales
John —— ——	"	Clerk to Desanque
B. A. M Thomas	"	Killed in Alamo

See Certificate of B. Lockhart on the 'original' for these names.

The foregoing list is not included in the general certificate Feb. 17, 1839.

A list of the Gonzales Ranging Company of Mounted Volunteers, mustered into service on the 23d day of February, 1836, by Byrd Lockhart, acting commissioner for that purpose and aid-de-camp to the acting Governor of Texas, attached to Travis' command:

NAME	RANK	REMARKS
George C. Kimbell	Lieutenant	Killed
William A. Irwin	1st Sergeant	
Jesse McCoy	Private	Kille
William Fahbaigh	"	Killed
John G. King	"	Killed
Daniel McCoy, Jr	"	
Jacob Durst	"	Killed
Frederick C. Elm		
Prospect McCoy		
M. L. Sewell	"	Killed
Robert White	"	Killed
John Ballard	"	
James Nash	"	
William Morrison	"	
Galba Fuqua	"	Killed
A. Devault	"	Killed
John Harriss	"	Killed
Andrew Kent	"	Killed
Isaac Millsaps	"	Killed
William E. Summers	"	Killed
David Kent		
John Davis	"	Killed

To these Mrs. Candelaria adds the following Mexicans:

Jose Marera Cabrera, Tula, Mexico.   Jose Maria Jimenes, Mexico.
Elijio or Elias Losoyo, San Antonio.   ——Jacinto, from the coast of Texas.

These make 169 slain.   Dr. Sutherland stated 172.

ADJUTANT GENERAL'S OFFICE, }
Austin, March 11, 1850.   }

I hereby certify the foregoing to be true copies of the original muster rolls now on file in this office.

BEN F. HILL,
Adjutant General.

Certificates from James S. Gillett, Adjutant General, dated March 19 and December 29, 1853, attached to copy of muster roll now on file in this office, show that Micajah Antry and Lewis Duel were killed at the Alamo.

GENERAL LAND OFFICE, }
Austin, Texas, March 30, 1889. }

I, R. M. Hall, Commissioner of the General Land Office of the State of Texas, hereby certify that the above and foregoing is a true and correct copy of the copy of the names of those who fell at the Alamo on the 6th of March, 1836, now on file in this office.

In testimony whereof, I hereunto set my hand and affix the impress of the seal of said office this March 30, 1889.

R. M. HALL,
Commissioner.

Jonathan Linly, fell at the Alamo, vouched for by J. D. Parker, of Birdville, Tarrant county, Texas, as per his letter to the Association, dated October 23, 1892, and on this statement the name of Jonathan Linly will be placed on the Alamo monument.

ALAMO MONUMENT ASSOCIATION,
H. P. BEE, Sec'y.

Alamo Monument Association.

SAN ANTONIO, TEXAS

CHARTERED BY THE STATE OF TEXAS

MRS. MARY A. MAVERICK .... PRESIDENT

NATHANIEL MITCHELL......... .... VICE PRESIDENT

JOHN S. FORD ....VICE PRESIDENT

HAMILTON P. BEE........................... ...SECRETARY

DIRECTORS.

W. H. YOUNG,	JAMES McMASTER,
MRS GEO. NEWTON,	MRS A. J. DIGNOWITY,
MRS. GEO CHABOT, SR,	SAM MAVERICK,
MORRILL POOR,	R. B. GREEN,
C. L. DIGNOWITY,	CARLOS BEE,
BRYAN CALLAGHAN,	SAM LYTLE,
ARTHUR SEELIGSON	HART MUSSEY.

Published by authority.

H. P. BEE,
Sec'y Alamo Monument Ass'n.

CPSIA information can be obtained at www.ICGtesting.com
Printed in the USA
LVOW10s1730160916

504958LV00017B/667/P

9 781331 388593